SAN FRANCISCO

SAN

Text by
Thomas Page

Minerva

FRANCISCO

Credits : Armytage/Photo-Researchers : 65 - Barnes/Photo-Re-
searchers : 7 - 14 - 26 c - 27 - 30 b - 52 b - 67 b - 86 - Biggs/Photo-
Researchers : 18 a - Carter/Photo-Researchers : 91 b - 112 - Curt-
singer/Photo-Researchers : 51 b - Davis/Photo-Researchers : 24 -
49 - Fiore : 28a, b - 29a, b - 50a - 53b - 79b - 90a, b - 91a - 108 -
109b, c, d - Georgia/Photo-Researchers : 9 - 93 - Gillette/Photo-
Researchers : 15 - Grehan/Photo-Researchers : 4 - 17 - 26d - 33 -
47 - 52a - 64b - 71 - 84b - 85 - Grunzweig/Photo-Researchers :
8 - Hanley/Photo-Researchers : 26a - 50b - 105a - Isear/Photo-
Researchers : 3 - Kinne/Photo-Researchers : 53a - Lefteroff/Photo-
Researchers : 39 - Levart/Photo-Researchers : 54a - Lowell/Photo-
Researchers : 64a - Lyon/Photo-Researchers : 48 - 78 - Mathey/
Vloo : 18b - 68 - 88 - 106 - 111 - Munitoz/Photo-Researchers :
25b - Munroe/Photo-Researchers : 70 - 100 - 101 - Namuth/Photo-
Researchers : 75 - 110 - Rowan/Photo-Researchers : 26b - 45a -
46 - 51a - 66 - 73 - 74 - Slaughter/Photo-Researchers : 104 - 109a -
Shumsky/Fotogram : 12 - 21b - Stokes-rice/Photo-Researchers :
42a - Van Bucher/Photo-Researchers : 23b - 79a - 89a - 92 - 98 -
107 - Vignes : End-Papers : 11 - 13 - 19 - 21a - 22 - 23a, c - 25a -
30a - 31a, b, c - 32a, b - 34a, b - 35 - 36 - 37 - 38a, b - 40 - 41a,
b - 42b - 43 - 44a, b, c - 45b - 54b - 55 - 56a, b - 57 - 58 - 59 -
60a, b - 61a, b - 62 a, b - 63 - 67a - 72 - 76 - 77a, b - 80 - 81a,
b, c - 82a - 83a, b - 89b - 94 - 96 - 97 - 103 - 105b - Wells Fargo
Bank : 31a, b, c - Wolff/Photo-Researchers : 69 - Zent Maier/Photo-
Researchers : 6 - 84a.

ISBN 0 517 241153

© Editions Minerva S.A., Genève, 1977

1.

It began as an earthen concussion on the seabed, under forty fathoms of water, whose shock waves buckled the keel plates of ships and tumbled crewmen violently out of their bunks. By the time they dashed to their portholes, the calm sea was littered with the carcasses of fish killed by the shock, drifting slowly to the surface.

From a point one hundred miles west of the shoreline, and ninety miles north of the Bay Area, it roared out of the ocean at a speed of seven thousand miles an hour, shattering and rocking the Point Arena lighthouse; then it veered south in a crazed zig-zag path that jumped in and out of the sea, derailing trains, shifting trees far from their roots and toppling others and killing livestock. An entire sawmill fell into a yawning split that opened up beneath it. A redwood tree was then deposited over it as a tombstone. Water and gas pipes split and burst deep underground. By the time it slammed under the city, San Francisco's reserve water supply was gone.

At 5:13 on the morning of April 18th 1906, while most of the city residents stirred under their sheets against the soft dawn light, the greatest recorded natural catastrophe to hit the North American continent struck the city of San Francisco. From every-

where rose the clanging of church bells ringing of their own accord, accompanied by the thunderous cracks of splitting masonry and collapsing buildings.

A police sergeant on morning duty saw it come down Washington Street "as if the waves of the ocean were coming towards me, billowing as they came". From his studio high atop Russian Hill the painter Bailey Millard gaped as the entire city rocked back and forth as if being pushed into the bay.

South of Market Street the three-foot waves of earth suddenly stopped rolling. Ten seconds of terrifying silence followed; then the second and third shocks burst over the shattered, toppling city and the fires began from thousands of leaking gas mains.

Enrico Caruso's manager ran into the singer's Palace Hotel suite to find the tenor sitting bolt upright in bed, eyes bulging in terror, his forty pairs of boots and loads of clothing scattered from fallen dressers across the floor. The manager ordered the frightened singer to try his voice out the window and calm the panic-stricken crowds below. After several false starts Caruso managed to sing, his clear, pure tones softening the disastrous bedlam below. It is said to have been the greatest performance of his life.

Brigadier General Frederick Funston, War Hero, Medal of Honor winner, Commander of the Presidio Garrison, which was one of

5

the oldest military forts on the continent, watched a forest of flames roar up on Market Street. He remembered how thirty-five years before, in the great Chicago Fire, another war hero, Phil Sheridan of the Union Army, had been asked to send troops into the city to keep order. On his own authority, Funston moved into action, alerting over two thousand soldiers housed at the Presidio and Fort Mason and immediately placed the city under martial law. The city administration had been corrupted by Mayor Eugene Schmitz and Abe Ruef who had looted profits from the restaurants and the vice areas of the Tenderloin and Barbary Coast. Long after the fire had died down and investigations were completed, the looting, vandalism and terror caused by Funston's own men would add to the annals of terror in old San Francisco, and whether the General had behaved properly or not is still a question debated by historians.

A.-P. Giannini, founder of the Bank of Italy with the support of the fruit and vegetable vendors of the city, informed his staff that the destruction had left the bank with only eighty thousand dollars to cover deposits of over a million. The money was in the form of gold buried under Giannini's living room floor. The next two months would determine their futures. There would be no staff holidays, sick leaves or time to pull their records together. Two barrels and a plank would serve as teller's cages, and the bank would make high-risk loans of five thousand dollars to anyone needing funds to rebuild. In fifty years Giannini's Bank of Italy would become the Bank of America, the largest in the world, and Giannini would die worth only five hundred thousand dollars, believing it to be enough money for anyone.

And in his own hotel room the actor John Barrymore awoke to find the lady who had shared his quarters was gone. Years later he

claimed he had never even known her name.

Although the quake was frightful enough, it was actually the subsequent fire that destroyed most of the city. For months afterwards relief funds, free food and help poured in, while refugees poured out. The totality of the disaster was complete. San Francisco, America's Pacific seaport, the glittering, barbaric, beautiful and matchless city of the Golden Gate, was annihilated. The San Francisco of today is a city scarcely seventy years old.

Some wondered if, by divine accountability, San Francisco had not called the wrath upon itself. Savagery and beauty existing side by side had long been the city's dominant personality. It was praised for its French, Chinese and Polynesian chefs and damned for the poverty of Chinatown and for the Barbary Coast press gangs who kidnapped men for duty aboard the ships moving in and out of the seaport. San Francisco's animal spirits, its headlong love of the good things in life, seemed to many like hedonism run rampant and perhaps quite a few secretly hoped the city was gone for good.

Left, a flower-vendor, one of many on the streets of San Francisco. Right, a striking example of the stark contrast between architecture of the past century and the latest modern styles.

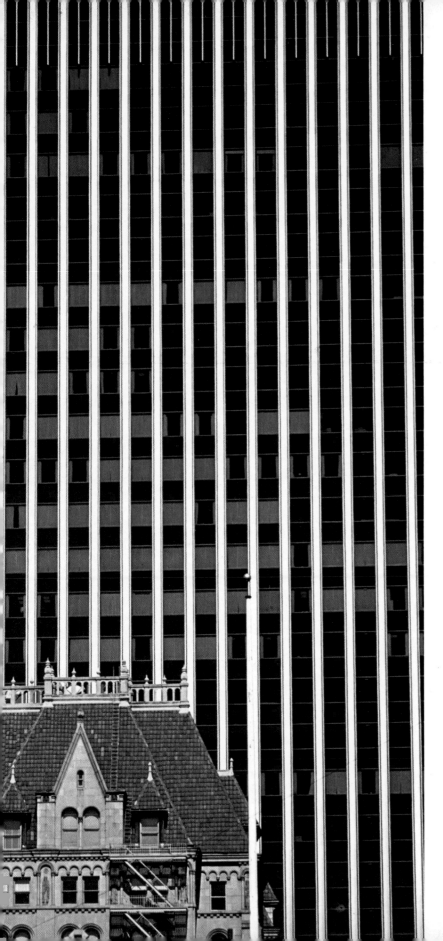

2.

San Francisco is located on a peninsula enclosing San Francisco Bay on one side and bordered by the Pacific on the other. Perhaps because near-daily fogs obscure the small strait connecting them, the great sixteenth century explorers kept missing it. The Spaniard Juan Rodriguez Cabrillo arrived first in 1542. Then in 1759 the English buccaneer and queen's favorite Sir Francis Drake made a landfall at Point Reyes north of the city and left behind a brass plate discovered in 1936. It's on view at the University of California Library in Berkeley. For two hundred years only Indians wandered about the Bay Area, then eighteenth-century power politics took a hand. Russia began colonizing Alaska in the north while the Spanish Empire held sway over the American west. Although the Russians were only seal hunters and furriers, the Spanish King Charles ordered California colonized before Russia or its rival England moved in. By then San Francisco Bay had become a legend known in ancient Portuguese as *Baia de Magnificencia Tremenda.* Don Gaspar de Portola finally discovered it in 1796, putting it on maps; but he was evidently unimpressed, for he formed a colony down the coast at Monterey. The City's actual founders were two Mexican Spaniards, friars of the Franciscan

9

Order named Junipero Serra and Fermin Lausen, who founded a string of missions up the coast from San Diego to Sonoma, along the route now called El Camino Real. These missions were the origins of the State of California which not only attracted colonists but spread the Catholic faith among huge numbers of Indians. Upon the little peninsula an English botanist named the sleepy village Yerba Buena, "good herb". The harbor itself was called San Francisco.

The Spanish Empire faded in the early 1800s and the Indians regressed to paganism. Little more than a thousand ranchers and seamen lived in the village of Yerba Buena by the 1840s. The massive holdings of the Spanish in the New World were lost in the Mexican War of 1846.

In 1839 at Fort Ross up the coast there occurred a tiny event of the sort which often proves to be a lynchpin on which history turns. The fort was sold to a Swiss army captain named Johann Augustus Suter in exchange for four years of food. Suter arrived from Hawaii, changed his name to Sutter and renamed the place Sutter's Fort. In 1849 a hired hand noticed odd colored stones in the stream and informed his friends that gold had been discovered. It was a magnet that shook the world and the next few years beggar description. Within one year forty thousand people descended from all over the world into the "mother lode" counties of San Francisco and its environs. That year the group of shanties and huts comprising Yerba Buena burned down, then burned down again six times in the next year and a half. It is certain the world will never see anything like the Gold Rush again. Rudyard Kipling marvelled at "what enchantment from the Arabian nights can equal this evocation of a roaring city in a few years... from the marshes and blowing sands". The city filled with brigands, bandits and poets of every description; Australian convicts, Cantonese boatmen, Latin American freebooters, Chinese railroad workers, Cornish tin miners, riverboat gamblers from the Mississippi, Hungarians, Frenchmen, Swedes and above all the hustling, cold-eyed, dollar-smart Yankees who rounded Cape Horn in South America or trekked across the Isthmus of Panama.

In those days an egg cost three dollars, Hawaiian pineapples cost fifty and the ship traffic was so heavy that the inhabitants sent their laundry to China. San Francisco became a collection of bordellos and free corps soldiers all looking for gold. Towns with names like Whiskey Diggings, Poverty Hill, Poker Flat (later immortalized by Bret Harte) and Bedbug sprang up in the Mother Lode. In one six-year period a thousand murders were recorded (easily only half of the number actually committed) and only one

man was convicted. Committees of Public Safety sprang up in the city to fight the huge criminal gangs that arose after the fires. They were called Vigilance Committees or "Vigilantes" who tried and hanged people more enthusiastically than the feeble courts did.

In order to prevent confusion with a new town called Francisca, the Chief Magistrate published a proclamation allowing use of the name San Francisco for Yerba Buena. And to further beggar belief, the most amazing event was happening by the end of the first half of the nineteenth century. Out of this lethal vulgarity, this cauldron of riffraff, gold hungry miners and bordello lovers, grew a city as famed for its sophistication as its boisterousness. From both sea and land arose a brand of cuisine famous for its variety and quality and from its houses came some of the most famous writers and artists the coun-

try has ever produced: Frank Norris, Jack London the firebrand socialist author of *The Sea Wolf* and *The Call of the Wild,* the poet and short story writer Bret Harte, and the Missouri migrant Samuel Langhorne Clemens whose tales about the Mother Lode were published first under his pen name of Mark Twain.

This was gold of a different type. Because of the rush, California, the furthest of the western states, was the first to be settled and San Francisco became the anchor of the trade, shipping and railroad wealth that appeared.

After the quake, the civic spirit was one of defiance. A businessman poet termed the smashed city the "damndest, finest ruins", and San Francisco rebuilt with breathtaking energy, along the Neo-Classical lines made *de rigueur* after the Chicago Exposition of 1893. Within days the disaster was called

Above and following pages: two samples of early architecture in San Francisco.

"The April Misfortune".

Three years later a Christmas concert was held at Lotta's Fountain on Market Street by the singer Luisa Tetrazzini. The city of the Golden Gate was back in business.

Since then the massive migrations centered around the war years, when San Francisco and other West Coast ports embarked troops to the Pacific and shipbuilding and aircraft plants appeared. Large numbers of these millions of people heading west for work found the climate and locale beautiful and stayed. Today the Bay Region is one of the most heavily populated in the world. California as a whole became America's most populous state in 1963 and as of 1974 an astonishing one of every two San Franciscans was foreign-born or had one parent of foreign stock. There are over thirty foreign language papers; and Chinatown, a city within the city, is the largest enclave of Chinese citizens anywhere in the United States.

It has been an uneven development. Many of the areas incinerated by the Great Fire—the Western Addition, Van Ness Avenue and south of Market Street—were different in character when rebuilt. For example, Van Ness, once lined with mansions, is now given over to the automobile age. South San Francisco is heavily industrialized and thousands of architectural wonders familiar to the literary days are gone forever. But the city's ambiance has increased rather than decreased. If the days of Mark Twain are gone then it can fairly be said that they have been replaced by such activities as the heavy rock music of the 1960s. It is said that California can expect another quake any minute. If so San Francisco is likely to rear its glittering head up once again even if all of California falls into the ocean. San Franciscans never give up.

One of the unique features of San Francisco is the way a kind of individual life-style has managed, despite being somewhat cramped, to fit harmoniously into a city in which the scale of dimensions is most definitely American.

3.

The rebuilding of the city after the April Misfortune followed a fairly simple plan: to apportion out the city in grids of blocks as nearly square as possible, much in the manner of other cities, like New York. Until the advent of Functionalism, the Columbia Exhibition of 1893 in Chicago had exemplified the most popular civic architecture in America. The exhibition displayed the building theories of the "City Beautiful", which in practice meant Neo-Classical structures, eclectified to remind citizens of ancient Rome and Greece. "City Beautiful", meant columns, imposing archways, domes, terraces, great avenues and miniature Parthenons. Square blocks would emphasize this theory admirably and San Francisco opted mostly for Beaux-Arts and Neo-Renaissance in its buildings.

The grid plan exists with unique variants. As anyone who has visited the city knows, San Francisco is built on hills. No-one is sure quite how many there are—estimates are between forty and forty-three—so laying a grid plan over these slopes leads to some aerial anomalies. Some houses appear to float in the air—altogether a delightful vista. Market Street, one of San Francisco's major thoroughfares, slants off southwest to northeast. The major objection to the grid plan was that it seemed square blocks served only real estate developers. Housing has waxed and waned from crisis to crisis in the city and everyone scrambled to get on a hill. Actually an effort has to be made to find an unpleasant view. The city gleams white under the sun, and sea breezes continually scrub pollution from the air and maintain a year-round temperature between 45 and 75 degrees Fahrenheit.

The center of the city is usually acknowledged to be Christmas Tree Point and Twin Peaks at the southwest end of Market Street. Around here lies the major concentration of business and commercial enterprise.

Market Street was founded in low comedy. It was surveyed by a villain named Jaspar O'Farrell in 1847. That O'Farrell was a Philadelphian was irritating enough. That he named it Market Street after Philadelphia's Market Street was insulting. That he compounded this sin by making it a full hundred twenty feet wide, thus cutting into lots owned by speculators, was infuriating enough to inspire a mass meeting of enraged city residents who forced O'Farrell to literally flee the city for his life.

Market Street today is an odd collision of past styles and present functionalism. It is sometimes called "The Slot" because of the cable car grooves set into the pavement. Cable cars may be San Francisco's single enduring symbol, an archaic means of transportation that has survived earthquakes and urban modernizing. The cable car was invented by a University of California regent named Andrew S. Hallidie, a wire and rope manufacturer who conceived the idea of separating the vehicle from its power source. The most common form of transportation in the nineteenth century was horse-drawn trolley. San Francisco's hills made this a dubious means of getting around. Hallidie caused small slots to be dug in the city streets into which was placed a continuously moving steel cable. The conductor activated a lever in the cable car which gripped the cable, allowing the machine to be dragged uphill. The invention was tremendously successful all over the country and became common in every major American city until the 1890s when the electric trolley made them obsolete.

Today there are only three cable car lines left but the brightly painted, bell-ringing machines are still in heavy use. San Franciscans are loath to terminate them despite the construction of a modernized transit system, and tourists still flock to the turntables to watch them turn around, or stroll through the cable car museum on Geary Street. As of this writing the cost of a ride is still a quarter and there are few better ways of getting around.

At the beginning of Market Street, the Embarcadero Freeway—one of San Francis-

The Palace of Fine Arts: continuing the finest neo-Classical traditions of the past century.

Above, Embarcadero Freeway.

co's capitulations to the automobile—passes a historic structure almost lost in the maze of the World Trade Center. The Ferry Building was one of the first sights immigrants and tourists saw of the city before the ferries were replaced by bay bridges. With its Seville cathedral tower, the building was not badly damaged by the quake although the clock hands stopped the instant it struck. Among the Ferry Building's attractions is, quite literally, gold. Gold nuggets, ore samples of uranium and copper are on display here in one of the country's largest mineral exhibits, testimony to the wealth of the earth that attracted so many.

Further up Market from the Ferry Building is Marine Plaza, a quiet little glade of a park in the midst of the city. How it manages to be quiet is something of a mystery since it is bordered by the modern Southern Pacific Building. Marine Square is a historic place on account of San Francisco's four most famous citizens—Collis Huntington, Charles Crocker, Leland Stanford and Mark Hopkins.

The Big Four brought far more wealth to San Francisco than could be dug from the ground. They were railroad barons, major performers in America's only epic adventure, the winning of the West. The American West quite literally ran on rails. In 1860, an Easterner named Theodore Judah interested the Big Four in a gigantic project; a transcontinental railroad linking the two oceans that flank America. The group incorporated into the Central Pacific and Judah laid a bet with a Vice-President of the Union Pacific that he could lay more track in a single day than his rival. With a crew of over 14,000 men, most of them Chinese, Crocker laid his track over the Donner Pass, the site of a wagon train disaster in which blizzards had once reduced a group of settlers to cannibalism. Crocker met the Union Pacific at Promontory Point in Utah where the last link was driven in with a golden spike. Marine Plaza shoulders up against Nob Hill where the Big Four built their mansions. The California Street cable car line from the plaza was built for their convenience to make it easier to get home from the office.

Mechanics Square was once the site of Yerba Buena Cove where gold was discovered in 1848, and it was here that a two thousand foot wharf fingered into the bay. A bronze plaque set into the sidewalk commemorates it. *Not* commemorated is the fact that the Market Street wharf was the gallows site from which the first Vigilante Committee hanged some of its victims. Douglas Tilden's sculpted Mechanics Monument on the northeast end honors a man named Porter Donahue, whose Union Iron Works was one of the city's first successful manufacturing concerns. The rest of the square is a mix of past and present sometimes combined into a single structure.

The Crown Zellerbach Building is a cantilevered, crystallized marine green fantasy of a building rising from columns around which is a sunny, light airy plaza in which multitudes of workers sit and eat lunch while catching a bit of sun. The Standard Oil Building is more in the tradition of pre-modern eclecticism: a steel-framed skyscraper encrusted with Italian Renaissance detail, it contrasts only a little with the Gothic detail of its competitor Shell Oil, on the North Side.

This kind of self-conscious reach into the past is not so much unusual taste as confused taste. Skyscraper construction arose from mid-nineteenth century experiments with cast iron and other materials, and it took time before appropriate styles could be found to match new methods of construction. Rather than jarring, the colliding mass of styles is playful in its effect.

The Pacific Gas and Electric Company's Beaux Arts building on Market Street is decorated with bighorn rams' heads and sculptures of linemen and construction workers. For a city so far removed from Europe and the East, it is curious that PG & E is believed to have been the first in the world to offer public electric service to its customers. It was available in 1879, a full three years before such a service was available in either London or New York.

Although San Francisco's shopping areas are diffused throughout the city, Market Street as well as the streets branching off from it are considered some of the busiest in the city. Each spring Union Square blos-

The Francis Drake *and* St. Francis *Hotels. Far right, a flower vendor on Powell Street.*

soms with rhododendrons. It was the site of mass rallies in favor of joining the Union during the Civil War and remains to this day a center for gatherings ranging from radical politicians to religious converts. Mostly it is used by pedestrians who enjoy the shade of the palms and the clipped green hedges. It is bordered by Neo-Renaissance buildings housing many elegant street-level shops ranging from boutiques to art galleries to airline offices. The city's fame as a center of rare and excellent stores comes largely from the Union Square area.

Felix Verdier was one of the French Republicans who, finding life in France uncongenial after Louis Napoleon's rise, emigrated to America bringing with him his fondness for French department stores. On the corner of Stockton and Geary Streets he founded the City of Paris store, whose basement keeps ample supplies of wines and specialty foods.

Magnin's was originally a small emporium opened in 1870 by Isaac and Mary Magnin for the sale of woodcarvings and baby clothes. An unsuspected talent for merchandising elevated the efforts of the two Dutch immigrants into a huge global chain of stores famed for women's wear. The marble building on Stockton and Geary Streets, built in 1948 as a "modern version of a Bohemian girl's dream of marble halls", has been imitated in many other cities.

The St. Francis and Sir Francis Drake hotels on Powell Street are two of the city's more famous establishments for visitors and pub lovers. The St. Francis has several murals by Alfred Herter including one with a figure of a woman named California. The model was the novelist Gertrude Atherton.

Sutter Street branching off Powell is also noted for its many specialty shops, in particular jewellers, antique dealers and art galleries many of which specialize in oriental ware. Podesta Baldocchi's flower shop on Geary and Powell Streets has been going since 1909. They change their window displays twice a day. Baldocchi's came to the rescue of the city's sidewalk flower vendors several years ago when moves were made to close them down.

West of Union Square on Post Street lies one of San Francisco's most outstanding stores. Gump's was founded, in 1861, almost by accident when Solomon Gump, a dealer in mirrors, picture frames and gilt cornices, sold some porcelain ware which had been piling up in the family parlor. Overnight he found himself in the interior decorating business.

Gump's originated the fashion of hostess pajamas in the 1920s when Mrs. A.L. Gump wore some of the store's pajamas to the French Riviera beaches. Today it deals in

everything from jewelry, pictures frames, (they were the first dealer in San Francisco of Currier & Ives prints) to glass, silver, housewares and particularly oriental art. The third floor ceiling is painted in watercolor images depicting four musicians who represent the four seasons. On continual display is the store's collection of jade, "the stone of truth and loyalty", along with other precious and semi-precious stones.

The stretch of Market Street between Mechanics Square and the Civic Center is

Left: Gump's. Opposite and below, the Palace Guard Court in the Sheraton Palace Hotel.

an area in constant flux, where the raucous present overwhelms the past. The Sheraton Palace Hotel has stood at New Montgomery since 1909, and Lotta's Fountain has survived both the earthquake and the passage of time. Lotta Crabtree was an actress beloved by the gold miners. The fountain was originally a watering trough for horses, then it was transformed into one for people. It was here that Luisa Tetrazzini sang Christmas carols to the crowds and celebrated the re-opening of the city after the quake.

Two views of the banking district. Right, the past lives again at the fascinating Wells Fargo Museum.

4.

San Francisco's financial district, nicknamed the "Wall Street of the West", backs up against Market Street and runs for some seven blocks along Montgomery, branching off into adjoining blocks. The City's original finance was based, not too surprisingly, on gold. The early banks were nothing more than repositories of gold dust for the miners. The first mint was established in 1854 and paper money was distrusted by the citizens roughly up to 1870.

Everyone who has seen a Western movie remembers a stagecoach being attacked by Indians or robbed by bandits. Almost always the name Wells Fargo is emblazoned across the coach. There really was a Wells Fargo Express company and its present quarters are located at Market and Montgomery. Wells Fargo originated in the capitalistic East on Wall Street in 1852 when William Fargo and Henry Wells established an express company that would span the continent from New York to San Francisco. Their mail and package delivery system was so safe that miners trusted it with gold.

Considering the bank's history it is not surprising that it is generally considered a conservative institution. Besides Indians and train robbers, the bank held on through financial crash after crash, many of which

were engineered by its rivals. The Express Company disappeared into the giant American Express Company and the bank itself became part of the American Trust Company. The fabled name Wells Fargo still appears on armored cars in which banks transport funds from one place to another.

The bank maintains a museum in its history room on Montgomery Strees in which one can get an impression of life in the Gold Rush days. It's a fascinating collection of everything from gold nuggets, frontier maps and stamp collections, to a stagecoach shipped around Cape Horn in the 1850s and

the scales said to have weighed 55 of the 87 million dollars in gold pulled from the Mother Lode.

The Crocker Anglo bank is not so famous but its roots run deep in San Francisco's turbulent past. It originated in London and combined with the railroad fortune of Crocker in 1873. After that it was a story of breakup and reconvergence, over and over again, through a history involving Alaskan fur traders and the expulsion of all foreign-owned banks from California in 1909. The building itself is a huge Neo-Renaissance revival edifice built by William Polk, one of the city's better-

Above, the entrance to the Mills Building. Below, the Stock Exchange. Right, view of California Street.

known local architects.

The Romanesque marble portal of the Mills Building is considered one of the architectural attractions of the area. The building survived the quake but the fire left traces inside, some of them still discernable. Carved decorations, including a pair of handsome monolithic statues, also enhance the Stock Exchange Building at Pine and Sansome. The trading day is from seven a.m. to two-thirty p.m. in order to match the time difference with Wall Street, two thousand miles to the east. The exchange's trading room is adorned with bas-reliefs while the luncheon club room contains frescoes by Diego Rivera representing the rise of California's agriculture, mining and industry.

How far in dignity the financial area has

Above, an unusual view of the Bank of America Building. Below, an interesting mixture of styles on Commercial Street. Right, plaque at the corner of Clay and Montgomery Streets.

ON JULY 9,1846, IN THE EARLY MORNING, IN "THE DAYS WHEN THE WATER CAME UP TO MONTGOMERY STREET," COMMANDER JOHN B. MONTGOMERY—FOR WHOM MONTGOMERY STREET WAS NAMED—LANDED NEAR THIS SPOT FROM THE U.S. SLOOP-OF-WAR "PORTSMOUTH," TO RAISE THE STARS AND STRIPES ON THE PLAZA, NOW PORTSMOUTH SQUARE, ONE BLOCK TO THE WEST. TABLET PLACED BY THE NATIVE SONS OF THE GOLDEN WEST. 1915.

come can be seen by contrasting it with what it was. The aforementioned Bank of America is now at Pine and California Streets and bears little resemblance to the fruit and vegetable business in which Gianninni began his career. He was not only the first to re-open after the fire but the first to establish branch banking and electronic processing of checks. When the Federal Reserve building was erected on Sacramento and Sansome streets excavators discovered a few odd relics buried on the site. Some coins, burnt wood and a metal tag labelled *gin* were classed as the only remains of a ship named 'the Apollo, a floating hotel which caught fire in one of the numerous holocausts of 1851.

On Commercial Street the Davidson Building is one of the town's older survivors and was once the headquarters of a newspaper editor with the peculiar name of James King of William. King's paper was the *Evening Bulletin,* which led relentless crusades against the corruption and violence of old San Francisco. He was shot to death by a rival editor named James Casey. A Vigilante committee quickly formed, captured Casey and hanged him summarily with a gambler name Cora. The Committee, whose membership, names and identities were kept secret, immediately disbanded but in this way King's death resulted in the kind of violence he had deplored so long.

Clay Street goes back to 1846. At the southeast corner of Clay and Montgomery is a plaque marking the spot where Commander John B. Montgomery raised the flag from his ship the Portsmouth. Portsmouth Plaza is one of the city's oldest parks, dating back to the day of the *pueblo.* It contains a flagpole memorial to Montgomery and a tall shaft surmounted by a bronze ship dedicated to the writer Robert Louis Stevenson, who used to visit the plaza when he lived in the city.

Two famous buildings: 750 Montgomery Street (facing). — 720 Montgomery Street (right): the cosy and unusual headquarters of a famous attorney.

Two plaques at Montgomery and Merchant Streets mark another memory of the westward move in America. Here was the terminal of the pony express, a tradition similar to that of the stagecoach, although the San Francisco route lasted barely a year. The Pony Express began in St. Joseph, Missouri. Riders travelled by horseback, carrying mail at the astounding rate of a hundred miles a day at full gallop, changing horses every fifteen or so miles.

Montgomery Street contains remnants of the past, some of which exist in the memory of San Franciscans more than in actual substance. Nevertheless the Montgomery Block at 628 Montgomery Street, also known as the "Monkey Block", somehow managed to avoid being dynamited by Funston's army after the quake. It was built in 1853 by General H.W. Halleck with materials brought in from England and France and was considered the oldest of the city's "fireproof" buildings. A burlesque fraternity of gold miners calling themselves the "Order of E. Clampus Vitus" placed a plaque on the Washington Street corner of the building, and it was also here that a celebrated drink called Pisco's Punch was perfected. James King of William was brought here dying of Casey's gunshot wound. Yet the most persistent memory associated with the building is that of the Emperor Norton, one of San Francisco's most beloved madmen, in a city that seemed ruled by them. Norton was an Englishman who lost first his fortune then his mind. He would stalk the city in sword and uniform declaring himself Emperor of the United States and Mexico. Many of his imperial proclamations met with the fervent approval of the city, such as his decree that the Democratic and Republican parties should be dissolved and that bridges should be built across the bay. The city was extremely fond of this gentle eccentric, allowing him to eat, drink and attend theatricals for nothing and to draw checks of up to 50 cents on any city bank. When he died the city was truly saddened and his funeral in 1880 was quite elaborate. Norton's favorite saloon was located in the Montgomery Block.

Before landfill pushed the waters of the Bay away, San Francisco designed what were called *ship buildings.* These structures were designed around actual ships tied to what was then the shoreline. The Golden Era Building on Montgomery Street is the last of these structures, and here the writer Bret Harte wrote some of his early works.

The area known as Jackson Square is considered the furthest west of the old downtown section. Although not actually in the financial district, the square—named after President Andrew Jackson—undergoes periodic renovations to shake the memory of its being part of the notorious Barbary

Two views of Hotaling Place.

Coast. Some remnants of this "devil's acre", where dancehalls, bordellos and gambling parlors once flourished, still exist today. The cast iron pilasters at Hotaling Place, designed in the French Second Empire style, contained for many years immense stores of wholesale whiskey, which unaccountably escaped the Great Fire. They would have made a spectacular blaze. The old dancehall quarter was on Pacific Avenue and some of its buildings, with their plaster relief sculptures, still remain. Here the sailors were drugged and kidnapped at night and awoke to find themselves on a ship bound for Asian ports. The Barbary Coast was the origin of two ugly words in English. To *shanghai* a man meant to kidnap him as just described. The word *hoodlum* derives from the shout "Huddle them!" which gangs used to cry before descending upon some helpless citizen.

Above, City Hall.

5.

Before the earthquake San Francisco's city government was not of a type to provoke much admiration. One of the mid-century vigilante groups successfully frightened the city administration into an unusual fit of honesty that lasted until 1872, when government reverted to the bad old days. Corporate graft and bribery often shows up most glaringly in the awarding of city building contracts. The city hall, which, suspiciously, took twenty-five expensive years to reach completion, must have been quite impressive. Even more suspiciously, it was the only building demolished by the earthquake alone, which raises even more questions about construction methods.

The present civic center with its City Hall is Renaissance in design. The present City Hall began construction in 1912 after two years of trials in which the mayor and a veritable army of grafters went to prison. By any standard it is a spectacular success, particularly at night with the floodlights on it. The exterior is of granite, complete with colonnades and Doric pavilions, the interior is carved marble and sandstone embellished with winding staircases and balconies and a huge rotunda. A formal French garden and plaza complete the gorgeous complex, with tiled walks, flower beds and distinctively Californian touches of sycamore and olive trees. The dome is sixteen feet three inches higher than the Capitol dome in Washington and one of the more curious American touches in an otherwise classical look is the western symbol of a bull's skull set in the pavilion metopes.

The Civic Center contains many other

39

Below, left, the Civic Center. Right, the famous Seventh Street Post Office and the modern United States Mint.

notable establishments. San Francisco claims to be the first city in the country to have built its own opera house. The present one, decorated with Gobelin tapestries and sculpture around the proscenium, opened in 1932 with Lily Pons singing Tosca. Enrico Caruso would have loved it for its acoustics are famous the world over (not that Caruso needed acoustics.) It was here that the United Nations Charter was adopted, in 1945, by delegates from all over the world.

Nearby is the San Francisco Museum of Art, whose permanent collection includes works by Picasso, Braque, Henry Moore and Diego Rivera, the Mexican artist whose works grace so many other parts of the city. The collection is inside the War Memorial Building which honors the Americans killed in the world wars, the Spanish-American War and the Civil War.

The Public Library, which contains more than a million volumes, is quietly beautiful inside, with various murals of the State's history and scenery adorning the walls. Travertine marble enhances the entrance hall, staircase and main delivery room.

The phrase "South of Market" refers to the area parallel to Market Street itself. Once it was populated mainly by the Irish, and was a combination residential and commercial area, but the quake and fire destroyed it so thoroughly that little trace of its past now

remains. Most of it is now devoted to industrial enterprises but there are nevertheless some interesting points. St. Patrick's Church on Mission Street between 3rd and 4th streets has been called the most Irish church on the American continent. At the time the first parish was founded by Father Maginnis he was the only English-speaking priest in the city—a fact which may give some indication of what a gloriously confused city San Francisco was then. The present structure went up after the Great Fire, and is made of brick in a rough Gothic Revival fashion. The church's interior is green Connemara marble brought in from Ireland by one of its priests, Father Rogers. The Gaelic atmosphere is furthered by the artist Mia Cranwill who based the vestments and crucifix on designs dating back to the sixth and eighth centuries.

Again it was Italy which inspired the US Post Office on 7th and Mission Streets—a building which was strong enough to survive the fire. Artisans were brought over from Italy to decorate the interior with Pavonazza marble trimmed in glass mosaic.

There are two US Mints in San Francisco. The older one, at 5th and Mission Streets, belongs to the classical style emphasized by Thomas Jefferson, complete with Greek Revival decor. Much of the ornamentation has been removed because it was dangerously insecure. The new Mint at Duboce Avenue and Buchanan Street was considered

impregnable to intruders, standing as it did on a 100-foot cliff with foundations deep in solid rock and festooned with gun towers, tear gas lines, electric alarms and all manner of security devices. In 1939 two schoolboys slipped up the wall of this fortress, entered a ventilation window and threw out a copper plate just to see if it could be done.

The Mission District is the site of the earliest Spanish-speaking settlements and thus may be considered the origin of the city itself. Mission Street is a regular street but the term "district" implies the area following the old trail line from Yerba Buena village in the North to the Mission Dolores at 16th and Dolores Streets. One would think the church's continued existence in a distinctly *non*-Spanish city is something of an authentic miracle, until one realizes how many Catholics

must have descended on San Francisco in the days of the 49ers. The church's graveyard contains Irish, Italian and French parishioners as well as older Mexican and Spanish citizens.

The church was built in June of 1776, five days before the Yankees of the East passed the Declaration of Independence.

The church's full name is the Misión San Francisco de Asis. Don José Joaquín Moraga who founded the Presidio established it. In those days the area teemed with livestock milling around, women, children and Indian Catholic neophytes being instructed in the Faith on orders from Colonel Juan Bautista de Anza. Bautista de Anza found the small stream which he named "Dolores" after the "Day of the Sorrows," March 29th, the very day he surveyed the area. Mission Dolores is a small church which looks as though it is quailing from the gigantic city around it. It has gone through periods of decay and renovation and, despite its diminutive size, was considered a heroic feat of construction in its time. The building measures a hundred fourteen by twenty-two feet and the walls are four feet thick and made of adobe. The roof timbers are tied with rawhide and the joints are pegged. Quite a few of the workmen who built it were Indians, recently converted Catholics, and the most striking evidence of their handi-

43

On this page, assorted photos of St. Francis of Assisi.

work is the triangular patterns of painting on the ceiling. Francisco de Haro, Yerba Buena's first alcalde and Antonio Arguello, California's first governor lie in the cemetery. And, for reasons history prefers to keep obscure, James Casey and Charles Cora, the murderers of James King of William are buried here too, along with three members of the Vigilante Committee who hanged them.

Time and the pressures of human habitation have eroded many of Dolores' original features, particularly the roof. Next to the little mission is the Mission Dolores Basilica erected in 1916; it is notable for its Spanish Revival design and for the fact that it was the fourth church in America to be designated a basilica. (And the first one so named west of the Mississippi). Large numbers of Latin Americans now call the Mission District home, which means it may be returning to its original composition. It is not exactly the good old days of the Spanish Empire but the good Friar Junipero Serra would feel more at home today than anytime since the Gold Rush.

To most people a symbol of San Francisco would be the cable cars, the Golden Gate Bridge or one of the numerous hills. But there is one symbol that originated in the city which is not known by many people and which has taken over large segments of the world's imagination. Valencia Street in the

44

Mission District is where Denim clothing originated. A tailor named Jacob Davis, of Virginia City, Nevada, is said to have become irritated with a miner who kept returning his pants for repairs. Tired of resewing the numerous holes and tears, Davis decided to try some of the tools used for repairing horse harnesses on the pants and riveted the pockets and seams with copper. On a trip to San Francisco he met Levi Strauss of New York, a dry goods manufacturer who was so impressed with the toughness of Davis pants he built a factory in the city and put Davis in charge of it. Denims are often called Levis in America. They've been a staple for workingmen for well over a hundred years, for most of which you could only get them in the color dark blue. The style evolved through usefulness rather than fashion to the low-slung, tapered shape with its huge belt loops and patched, capacious pockets. The rivets were replaced by tough thread. Denims or Levis or blue jeans or whatever people call them are not exactly world-shaking inventions but they originated in San Francisco and that is as graphic an illustration of the city's fundamental sense of style as can be found.

The revolutionary forms of dress which swept through the youth of the entire world all started here: below, the famous blue jeans factory, Levi Strauss.

6.

San Francisco's Chinatown is quite literally a city within a city, an entity as old as the oldest to be found there. Ever awestruck by the anomalies of San Francisco, Rudyard Kipling called it a "ward of the city of Canton set down in the most eligible business quarter of the place." Estimates of the Chinese population of San Francisco are being constantly revised upwards. The 1960 census guessed at 36,000 Chinese and Chinese-Americans living in the area but a more recent estimate puts the number around a hundred thousand. Either estimate is a fair-sized city, by any standards.

Most of the original Chinese came to Gum Sahn (Golden Hills, as they called the Bay Area) in the Gold Rush. Most are descendants of the people of Kwangtun Province. The original immigrants were largely Canton boatmen who came to seek their fortune along with the rest of the world. There are some very dark undercurrents in the Chinese experience in San Francisco. They arrived as part of the "coolie" or labor trade, many to work on the western railroads. Although most was contracted labor, in actuality it was but a cut above slave conditions and the phrase "shanghaied" refers not only to practices on the Western side of getting crews on ships heading East but common

practices on the Canton waterfront as well. In those days, when China was at the mercy of the opium trade and foreign powers, labor was cheap.

Chinatown extends roughly for eight blocks down Grant Street. It has swelled and shrunk during the passage of time and evolved from a slum riddled with opium dens, white slavery and tong wars into a vibrant, glittering community replete with primary colors in its decor and fragrant smells from its cooking. Chinatown's food is famed the world over, as are its stores selling carved ivory, jewelry and other Oriental ware.

Grant Street has a bizarre history for reasons other than its association with Chinatown. It is recorded as the first street to be laid out in the city. The Spaniard Francisco de Haro named it Calle de la Fundación—Street of the Founding—in 1834. Shortly after the US conquest, it was renamed Dupont Street after an Admiral. After the Chinese began settling *Dupont Gai* it became so disreputable that Market Street merchants had the name changed to Grant Avenue. Whether this was an honor or an insult to President Grant is difficult to understand.

St Mary's Square on Grant and California Streets was once part of Chinatown's red light district. It is now a small grassy area frequented by children playing around a

48

steel and concrete statue of Dr. Sun Yat Sen. St. Mary's Church across the Square is a Gothic brick structure that contrasts sharply with the pointed Chinese detail of its neighboring buildings. The church was made from material brought round the Horn from China. An inscription on the clock reads "Son, observe the time and flee from evil."

Kong Chow Temple on Pine Street is the largest Chinese joss house in America and was dedicated to a military God named Kwan Ti, the patron of those who undertake hazardous work or adventures. It has two altars inside, one for morning tea and one supplied with pen and paper for writing down visitors' requests. The oldest joss house in the city is the Tin How Temple, which, because of a requirement allowing no human handiwork besides a roof to stand above the Gods, was situated on the fourth floor of the building.

Tin How was Queen of the Heavens and, more appropriately, Goddess of the Seven Seas whose original altar was on board a ship. And finally the more modern Buddha Universal Church houses a sect founded in San Francisco in 1910. The building combines Chinese simplicity with that of modern functionalism, particularly in the way wood is smoothly melded into the decor. The Sect's formal title is the Pristine Orthodox

49

Dharma and emphasizes practical truths to contrast against superstitions within the older sects.

Probably Chinatown's major attraction is its varied *cuisine*—the work of restaurants too numerous to count. Cantonese cooking was long the basis of the food served here, but in recent years people have been developing tastes for the spicier Szechuan fare.

The Bank of Canton is housed in what was once the Chinese Telephone Exchange. It is an ornate, triple-tiered building with a brightly painted roof. In the days when it was used for telephone calls, the twenty operators who worked there not only spoke English and the five Chinese dialects used in the city, they had memorized the numbers of over 2,100 subscribers.

Despite the canyon depths of Montgomery Street and the skyscrapers such as the Transamerica Pyramid, San Francisco presents a relatively low profile. It is a remarkably compact city with its many wonders within easy walking distance.

7

The hills are probably most challenging to a pedestrian. Three of the forty hills, Russian Hill, Telegraph Hill and Nob Hill have their own claims to fame.

Nob Hill was home to the men who dominated San Francisco's social and financial life during the gilded age, particularly the Big Four. Some of the social habits arose by accidents. Tradition has it for example that Eastern railroad barons who travelled around in private railway cars would never undertake a journey without their baths, bars and French chefs in attendance. Upon arriving in San Francisco, these chefs became so enraptured with the abundance of fish and game as well as the chance to begin their own business, that they abandoned their bosses and opened up their own restaurants, thus founding San Francisco's culinary reputation.

These restaurants proliferated through the Barbary Coast areas as well as the more expensive neighborhoods. A very popular dish around the turn of the century was Chicken *potrero,* devised by a San Franciscan and using chicken stuffed into a hollowed coconut shell baked in a cream, cheese and vegetable sauce and served fiery hot. Chinese, Japanese, French and basic American cuisine mixed very well sometimes

into combinations rarely seen today. Every sizable town in California seems to have a restaurant called the Poodle Dog. The first Poodle Dog was an elegant French establishment whose most direct descendant is over on Post Street. *Poodle Dog* is a nickname used by citizens who were unable to pronounce the real name, "Poulet D'Or", with proper Gallic pronunciation. Besides food, the Poulet d'Or, and a number of similar establishments, provided services of a somewhat more scandalous nature.

They were often subdivided into two sections—a common room for the average rich and special curtained booths allowing discretion for the above-average rich and whatever guests decided they should be entertained in a discreet manner. These booths were equipped with handsome spacious couches. They were accessible by private stairway and decorated with baroque velvet hangings, gold candelabras and silver dinner services. San Francisco catered in style to the most selective appetites.

The rich were often called "nabobs"—a bitter, derisive term from which the name Nob Hill arose. Nob Hill's name could not have come very early. Contemporary accounts of life in old San Francisco clearly indicate that despite the most appalling abuses of power by the wealthy, there was little class resentment. Everybody came to this city to strike it rich and so much wealth came so fast that the nabobs and the city coachmen remained on a first name basis. Class divisions simply did not have time to form. The rich and poor attended the same theatre, and ate in the same restaurants attended by the same waiters. The example of James Flood might illuminate this. Flood was a caretaker in a bar and carriagemaker who made a sudden fortune as a speculator. When he built his Nob Hill mansion of eastern brownstone, he surrounded it with a gold fence called by his drinking buddies "Flood's brass rail." Flood's mansion still stands today as the site of the Pacific Union Club, a men's organization so exclusive it has only 100 members. Times have definitely changed.

Soon after the cable car line up to Nob Hill was completed, Mark Hopkins, one of the Big Four, built a mansion, complete with a carriage house and retaining walls said to have been more costly than the building itself. The earthquake made short work of that and the site is occupied today by the Mark Hopkins Hotel or "The Mark" as San Franciscans call it. The Mark is an extremely handsome and graceful piece of work, a 1926 skyscraper gorgeously designed in Renaissance, Spanish and Baronial French, as befits a building commemorating a capitalist baron. The Room of the Dons

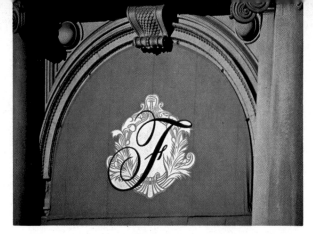

contains murals depicting the early history of California and there is a peacock court with a lunette of Leda and the Swan done in encaustic painting. One feature of the Mark has become world famous since World War Two. It is the top floor bar, which was a gathering place for servicemen who used to rendez-vous here before shipping off to the Pacific or Europe. The Top of the Mark is over five hundred feet above the Bay level and provides a smashing view of the city.

James ("Bonanza Jim") Fair made his fortune in Nevada's silver lode country and commissioned work on a huge mansion but died before it was finished. Plans were made to turn it into a hotel but the Great Fire gutted the building. Today's Fairmont Hotel is beautiful by any standards, with a generous assortment of bars and restaurants and a tiny theatre seating 20. Attractions such as the Terrace Plunge and the Circus Room are elaborately decorated with murals and a pair of rare 16th-century Florentine mirrors. On the northeast side is a brand new tower with an outside elevator San Franciscans have dubbed "The Thermometer," which leads to the bar on the summit, twenty-nine stories up.

Sad to say, little else of the original splendor of the nabobs remains on the hill. What remains has been either destroyed or reconverted. The estate of Leland Stanford

is now occupied by the Stanford Court apartment building with a sculpture of a penguin and her young by Benjamen Bufano. However Grace Cathedral, on California and Jones Streets, is certainly a spectacular presence. It is built on the grounds of Charles Crocker's home and occupies a full block of California Street. The church is the seat of the California Episcopal bishop, the third largest diocese in the country, and took many years to complete.

Grace Church is a veritable treasure trove inside—stained-glass windows by Charles Connic of Boston, Flemish altar decor and beautifully wrought woodcarvings and statuary. In the nave are murals by Henryk de Rosen, preserved in a wax emulsion to keep the colors bright. The models for the Indians in these murals are all too obviously Chinese. The Chapel of Grace in the south nave is a Gothic—styled place containing a tenth-century stone altar from Brittany and a carved stone credence table dating from the fourteenth century.

The dimensions of the church are the major reason it was under construction for so long. The highest nave in England, at Westminster, is 102 feet tall and the highest in Europe is the one at Beauvais Cathedral at 157 feet. Grace's is 300 feet high. Considering that the hilltop is 278 feet above

Above, inside Grace Cathedral.

sea level, the spire rises a full 500 feet above sea level.

Grace Cathedral contains a six-thousand-pipe Aeolian Skinner organ considered by many musicians among the best in the world. The 43-bell carillion in the west tower was cast in England.

Facing Grace Church is another large edifice of white marble gleaming brilliantly under the California sun. It's the California Masonic Temple, completed in 1958. Bas-reliefs and murals decorate the interior and exterior of the building and the temple has one of the city's best auditoriums.

8.

Telegraph Hill was once known as the art colony of the city. It's been a long time since prices here were low enough to keep the artists, writers and painters who once called it home. Since the end of the 1930s these people have found more appropriate housing in Sausalito and further down the coast.

Telegraph Hill is named for a semaphore which used to signal, by certain positions of its two large arms, what kind of ship was entering the bay. There is an apocryphal story about this semaphore. An actor appearing in a local theatre learned in an unusual way how expert San Franciscans were in reading the semaphore. In the middle of a difficult scene of high melodramatic tension, the performer turned beseechingly to the audience and cried out his next line: "But what does this mean?" with his arms held wide. Responding to his arms, the audience yelled back "Schooner!"

On top of the hill is a memorial to one of the city's most bizarre characters, Lillie Hitchcock Coit. When she was a girl she used to venture alone into the city and catch rats with string and cheese. Her pranks became more elaborate as she grew older. Upon passing her open window, students of the Lane Medical School were often startled

by one of Lillie's delicious bare legs protruding from an upstairs window and her voice crooning a popular music hall song "Doctor, dear Doctor come saw off my leg."

Lillie was called a phantom of delight by the citizens. She smoked cigarettes in public, drank with the dock loaders, was a sharp poker player and loved cock fights. In addition to her numerous passions, she had one that all but overwhelmed her. She was wild about fire engines.

In those days San Francisco was still occasionally devastated by fires. Long before a city Fire Department was formed, these blazes were put out by Volunteer Companies. They were colorful, fiercely independent organizations, with their own insignia, who raced each other to the disasters. Lillie attached herself to an organization called the Knickerbocker Engine Company Number 5. Whether she was attracted more by the rumbling horse drawn engines or by the firemen, is lost to History's discretion. She dashed off to blazes with the company and attended their annual banquets dressed in firemen's boots, black tie and a scandalously short dress—fully eight inches off the floor. She was made an honorary member and wore a gold pin with the Number 5 on it for the rest of her long life till she died in 1928. Among her close friends were artists and the writers Bret Harte and Robert Louis Steven-

son. Coit Tower, atop Telegraph Hill, is her memorial.

The tower was erected in 1933 under direction from the Federal Works Progress Administration and financed by bequests from Lillie. It is dedicated to the volunteer firemen. The pervasive talent of Diego Rivera produced some murals, for the interior of this building, which reflect the social turmoil of that decade. Another tribute to the firemen is a small bit of statuary in Washington Square. Perhaps the most famous message the semaphore ever received was in 1850 when the steamer *Oregon* entered the bay with word that California had been admitted to the Union. An enormous bonfire was built on top of the hill in celebration. Today the buildings are largely apartment buildings in varied stages of elegance where new apartment buildings nestle against clapboard and shingle old houses. The tower stands in the middle of Pioneer Park. The Hill's cliffs are actually man-made. Granite was quarried from it after the earthquake for building materials and continued all through the years until the 1950s when the city halted it.

Facing, San Francisco seen from the top of Telegraph Hill.

Picturesque Lombard Street and typical houses on Russian Hill.

9.

Russian Hill's tradition as a haven for artists is even older than Telegraph Hill's reputation. The name derives from the nineteenth century Russian sealers and hunters who were buried here. Like Telegraph Hill, it is now covered with apartment buildings and handsome homes.

It still has many startling vistas, such as the spiral gardens of Lombard Street which corkscrew up the hill in a brick-paved and beautifully landscaped fantasy, richly ornamented with hydrangeas. The architect Willis Polk, who built many of the outstanding buildings of old San Francisco, was a member of a group of artists called *Les Jeunes* that included the stained-glass artist Bruce Potter. Polk lived on Russian Hill and his own home on Taylor Street still stands. It is a brown shingled dwelling now subdivided into private apartments. Much of Polk's work was noted for simple exteriors which contrasted with surprisingly complex interiors.

One of the more peculiar rages in building in San Francisco was the erection of octagonal houses. On Green St. is a building dating back to 1855 shaped like an octagon, in keeping with theories propounded by a man named O.S. Fowler. For some reason Fowler believed octagon-shaped walls with gravel faces were good for one's health.

Exactly why he believed this and precisely how an eight-sided house is supposed to keep one alive longer is unclear, but the Fousier Octagon House, as well as another one on Gough Street, are testimony to the success he had in promoting this theory.

On Russian Hill's summit is a small park and memorial to a poet named George Sterling who, though he never really became famous outside of the city, was San Francisco's informal poet laureate. Some of Sterling's friends did become famous. Jack London was arguably the most popular writer on earth for several years at the turn of the century, and Ambrose Bierce had a fearsome reputation as a bitter, acidulous critic and even more cynical writer. Bierce vanished in Mexico.

The San Francisco Art Institute on Russian Hill's Chestnut Street has many innovations to its credit. This Italian Renaissance villa structure is the oldest art school west of the Mississippi and the first in America to teach photography as a Fine Art, under the instruction of the great nature photographer Ansel Adams. It originated abstract expressionism on the West Coast after World War Two and contains work by artists ranging from Diego Rivera to Mark Rothko. Robert Louis Stevenson dedicated *Silverado Squatters* to the school's founder Virgil Williams and his wife, in gratitude for the tutoring Williams did for his wife and daughter. The School is affiliated with the University of California and offers the degrees of Bachelor and Master of Fine Arts.

Left, what was once one of the centers of the Hippy movement. Right, the magnificence of Embarcadero Plaza.

10.

Night Life in San Francisco is not quite so dangerous as it was in Gold Rush days but it has its tawdry angles. North Beach running between Telegraph and Russian Hill is the center of it. North Beach has not been near water since 1881 when landfill created it.

North Beach is riddled with jazz caverns, topless bars and movie theatres particularly along the Broadway Strip. Although the Bohemian is often hard to separate from the raucous, it is certain that this area will never approach the lethal ambiance of the old Barbary Coast. In deference to its predominantly Italian, Spanish and Latin American residents, it's sometimes called the Latin Quarter of San Francisco.

San Francisco's Italian population dates back to the Gold Rush days. They came originally from northern Italy and were followed in the 1880s by Sicilians who gathered around Fisherman's Wharf. St. Francis Church was founded by a French community but its patrons have traditionally been Italian. Burnt out by the fire, the church's walls held firm and the interior was rebuilt along Gothic Revival lines. North Beach has many coffeehouses and bistros, where pedestrians can relax and watch the show on the sidewalks.

Grant Avenue north of Broadway was the

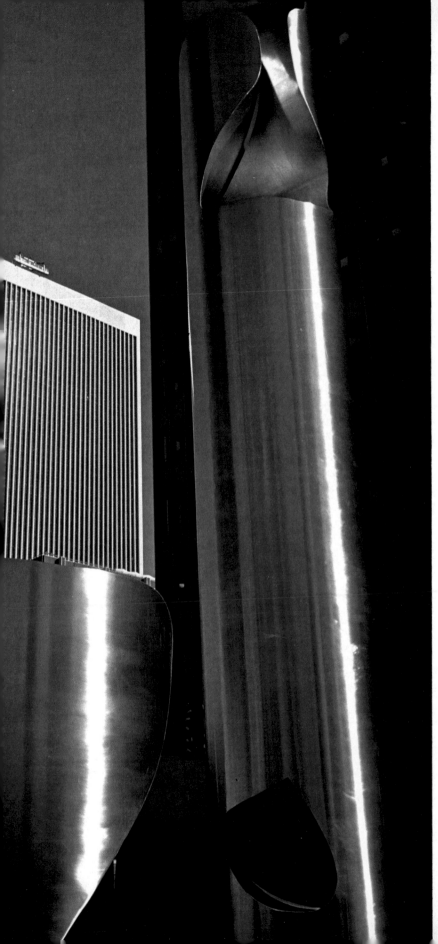

founding home of the Beatnik generation, the gentle, somber, eccentric poets whose lives in the 1950s prefigured the Hippies of the 1960s. The movement originated in San Francisco. One of its most distinguished remnants is the City Lights book-store on Adler Place, founded by the poet Lawrence Ferlinghetti who published special series devoted to poets such as Allen Ginsberg and novelist Jack Kerouac.

Over the years since 1906 a challenge more powerful than any earthquake has faced San Francisco. The automobile. There was little doubt about the automobile's utility in the state of California, where large tracts are desert flat and distances are enormous. The highway system is still being built, under a continuing plan financed at an estimated cost of some ten billion dollars. It is within the cities themselves that the auto has had its most questionable effect. The necessity of garages and freeways, where to put them and how to handle them presses hard upon city planners. The city's major freeways roughly bound the city on both bay side and ocean side alike. The Embarcadero Center and the Golden Gateway Center were built according to modern theories that group residential, commercial and leisure functions should be carefully integrated into the road system. The design impacts thus made on San Francisco's famous waterfront have been

Fountains on Embarcadero Plaza. Right, The Cannery, *near Ghirardelli Square.*

carefully controlled ones.

Ghirardelli Square is the site of a chocolate factory that has been renovated into a seductively beautiful complex of restaurants, art galleries, boutiques, taverns, all of which look out through fountains at the Bay Area.

Some views of Ghirardelli Square.

Facing, Fisherman's Wharf. Right, one of the local fish restaurants and a 16th-century craft at the Ship Museum.

San Francisco's most famous shore area is Fisherman's Wharf. The wharf was early set aside for use by the city's commercial fishermen, who were largely men of Chinese and Sicilian ancestry. Fisherman's Wharf, which protrudes into the bay, is an altogether delightful madhouse of Italian restaurants, live crabs and souvenir shops. Despite its 20th-century sophistication the city still needs the fishing boat fleets that glide out of the harbor at dawn.

Fisherman's Wharf lies between the Maritime Museum and a floating memento of the past, a square rigged Cape Horn ship called the *Balclutha*. *Balclutha* was built on the river Clyde and launched from Glasgow, Scotland, in 1886. Her maiden voyage was around the Horn to San Francisco and her history is largely that of part of the grain trading fleet. *Balclutha* is her most recent name, several others being *Star of Alaska* and *Pacific Queen*. She is a large steel-hulled ship measuring 256.5 feet in length and 38.6 at the beam. This exciting vessel is open to the public on Pier 43; it is certainly enough to make a child out of any adult.

In the Pacific Heights and Marina sections of San Francisco stand some of the city's most beautiful neighborhoods. Aquatic Park is a spectacular combination of ocean scenery and landscaped earth forming a semi-circle that encloses half a mile of water. It is San

Francisco's premier waterfront recreation area and encourages every kind of activity from swimming and boating to viewing several ships, now converted into floating museums, which lie close to the Hyde Street Pier. Sunday is a perfect day for visiting Aquatic Park with the sun glittering off the waters and the boats playing through. The Park was built by the WPA in 1939 and includes a ca-sino four stories high with its ends rounded like a ship's. The casino is an elaborately devised construction complete with murals, dining clubs and lounges with glass fronts facing the sea. Yet the major entertainment of San Franciscans is simply to come to the promenade with its stone bleachers and grassy expanses on which to nap, walk and otherwise soak up the sun.

Lincoln Park once was the site of the City's cemetery, which segregated the dead according to nationality. It must have been a pretty confusing area in view of the polyglot nationals who have called the city home. The Chinese cemetery is now a golf course whose first hazard is the sacrifice stone, an oven used for roasting pigs to placate the gods.

Those who lived in the Pacific Heights area built some of the city's most beautiful residential sections. Pacific Heights generally competes with Nob Hill for the reputation of center of the "beautiful people". Many of these residences are fully fledged estates, because of the obvious availability of land. Despite their careful (and expensive) adherence to Neo-Georgian, Victorian, French and Italian Palazzo styles, the early builders were Romantics. Some of their houses were amazingly eclectic. The Spraekels mansion, a white marble concoction, has more than once been compared to a large cake—a particularly apposite remark when one remembers that the Spraekel family fortune was made in sugar. In some sections the houses line the streets, for all appearances like any quiet residential neighborhood, save for their gigantic scale. Pacific Heights has managed to strike a balance with the builders of luxury apartments in the neighborhoods and some of them are open to the public. The California Historical Society Headquarters is housed in

a sandstone behemoth built in 1896 for a paint company executive. The interior amply demonstrates the tastes of the turn of the century.

One of the sections of Pacific Heights is Presidio Heights, named for the bordering Presidio Military Reservation (the oldest such establishment in the country). Two points of interest exist on Arguello Boulevard. One is a building, the other is a memory.

The building is Temple Emmanu-El, the city's center of Reform Judaism and home of the largest Jewish congregation in San Francisco. It is a large, handsome, cream-colored

Spraekels Mansion: in the best and most refined traditions of old Europe. Right, the superb Emmanu-El synagogue.

building of Byzantine design with a red tile dome, dating back to 1926.

The memory is that of a very beautiful girl named Concepción Arguello for whose family the boulevard is named. Her father was the Commander of the Presidio garrison. Concepción fell hopelessly in love with a Russian count named Rezanov who was on a visit to set up rights for a trading house. The couple carried on a passionate affair, with everyone's approval, until Rezanov returned to Russia. He promised to return and marry her.

She waited faithfully for him but no word came and apparently, broken-hearted, she entered a convent. She was there for thirty six years and it was only then that they learned Rezanov had not jilted her but had died on the boat back to Russia, and no one had thought to inform the family. Concepción's life appeared in stories by both Bret Harte and the novelist Gertrude Atherton.

83

It is impossible to imagine any city with a substantially wealthy class without some of that wealth being spent on yachts. Since San Francisco's soul is intimately tied up with the sea, it is not surprising that the citizens are mad about sailing, water-skiing and otherwise making use of the Bay for enjoyment.

The Bay is a veritable crossroads of sloops, Sailfish, Sunfish, cat boats with wide wallowing hulls and sleek motorized yachts. The first San Francisco Yacht Club was formed in 1869. Sailing goes on for most of the year, the bulk of the happy sailors being weekenders. There is an official season which begins on the first Sunday in May and continues for five months of sharp competitive sailing. San Francisco has over twenty-five yacht harbors including the municipal one. The two major clubs are the St. Francis and the Golden Gate. Other clubs are based at various places on the coast as well as the islands.

The Presidio is a fifteen-hundred-acre wooded military preserve founded in 1776 by the Spanish. It is from here Fort Mason that General Funston called his troops to the aid of the firemen and police in 1906. The Presidio was designed for the defense of the harbor and passage. It is the largest military establishment in any American city and, to a large extent because of the Army's help in housing the homeless on its ground for over

84

There are twenty five harbors
for sail-boats in San Francisco.

a year after the disaster, it has always been on good terms with the city residents. Before 1880 this section of land was barren sand dunes and rocky cliffs. In that decade a nationwide campaign got underway to beautify the nation's parks, so army engineers planted trees and foliage throughout the grounds. Many parts of the Presidio are open to those who enjoy walking through the forested lane.

Fort Winfield Scott on the northwest corner of the reservation is the actual site of the guns which were to protect the city in case of war. The guns were never used and the fort is abandoned today. The closest the Presidio has ever come to actual combat was the day in the nineteenth century when Lieutenant John C. Fremont stormed the cliffs, climbing all the way up into the line of fire of artillery only to learn the Spanish were no longer there.

The Officers' Club is on the site where Lieutenant José Joaquin Moraga first established the fort. This adobe structure built in 1776 is the oldest building still standing in the city of San Francisco.

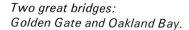
*Two great bridges:
Golden Gate and Oakland Bay.*

11.

The major San Francisco approach from the Presidio is one of the most spectacular engineering feats in the country, the Golden Gate Bridge. For many years it was the longest suspension bridge in the world—an honor since claimed by New York's Verrazano Bridge. With its reddish gold frame laced by spidery strands of steel, glowing with yellow lights at night, it still ranks as one of the most beautiful. The bridge was designed by one Joseph Strauss and went up during the Depression, after A.P. Giannini decided to buy up the bonds. Strauss called it the most difficult engineering feat ever undertaken. Some of the statistics about it are astounding.

The towers are 746 feet above water and the full length is 8,940 feet—close to a mile and a half. The supporting cables are three feet in diameter and consist of 27,572 individual strands of steel. The south pier rests on bed rock a full hundred feet underwater. When completed, the bridge's central section was almost two hundred fifty feet above water, high enough to allow the Queen Elizabeth to pass safely beneath at high tide. More impressive than these numbers are the numerous stories of heroism centering around its construction. The Gate of the Bay is notorious for the vicious currents that sweep in

Below, plaque commemorating the building of the Golden Gate Bridge. Facing, section of one of the suspension cables of the bridge. Right, traffic on the bridge, and a view of the bridge at nightfall.

DEDICATION
BY THE DIRECTORS
AND OFFICERS OF THE
GOLDEN GATE BRIDGE
AND HIGHWAY DISTRICT

IN THE YEAR 1937 NINETEEN YEARS AFTER ITS INCEPTION
THE GOLDEN GATE BRIDGE OF SAN FRANCISCO IS HERE
DEDICATED
TO THE PEOPLE OF THE GOLDEN GATE BRIDGE AND
HIGHWAY DISTRICT WHO GUARANTEED IT
TO THE CITIZENRY OF THE STATE OF CALIFORNIA
WHO SPONSORED IT
AND TO THE WORLD AT LARGE WHOSE ADVENTUROUS
SPIRIT IT REFLECTS

LIFTING ITS MIGHTY FORM HIGH ABOVE THE GOLDEN GATE
IT SHALL TESTIFY TO THE FAITH AND DEVOTION OF THOSE
WHO UNDAUNTED THROUGH THE YEARS
SOUGHT HONESTLY AND FAIRLY THROUGH THIS STRUCTURE
TO TENDER A DEFINITE CONTRIBUTION
TO THE CULTURAL HERITAGE OF MANKIND

CONCEIVED IN THE SPIRIT OF PROGRESS
IT SHALL STAND AT THE GATES OF SAN FRANCISCO
A MONUMENT TO HER VISION AN INSPIRATION TO
POSTERITY
AND AN ENDURING INSTRUMENT OF CIVILIZATION
FAITHFULLY SERVING THE NEEDS OF A QUICKENING WORLD

DEDICATION
BY
THE NATIVE SONS
OF THE GOLDEN WEST

AS A TRIBUTE TO THE ENGINEERING GENIUS
WHICH GAVE TO THE STATE OF CALIFORNIA
THE GOLDEN GATE BRIDGE
THE LONGEST BRIDGE SPAN IN THE WORLD
WE THE NATIVE SONS OF THE GOLDEN WEST
MAKE THIS DEDICATION
IN RECOGNITION OF
THE BEAUTY AND THE UTILITY
OF THIS GREAT STRUCTURE
AND THE SCIENTIFIC ACHIEVEME
FOR WHICH IT STANDS
MAY 27 · 1937

ONE HUNDRED AND FIFTEEN FEET SOUTHWARD FROM THIS PANEL ON THE CENTER
OF THE BRIDGE A STARRED DISK OF BRONZE MARKS THE CENTER OF THE OLD
CONTROL STATION OF BATTERY LANCASTER WHICH ONCE OCCUPIED THAT SITE
THAT POINT THE FIRST RECONNAISSANCE OF THE GOLDEN GATE BRIDGE WAS INITIA

and out with the tides four times a day, and there are legion stories of ships being smashed against caissons, whole sections tearing loose and constantly revised plans while it was being built. Among the lesser glories of the Golden Gate Bridge is that it is the only respectable place in the city to commit suicide. San Francisco police report an average of eight people a year take the final leap from it. Only one man is known to have survived the fall. There is an odd statistic connected with bridge suicides. Most jump from the San Francisco side of the bridge. City lovers say it is because they want their last sight on earth to be of the town. Others claim the suicides are afraid of crossing to the ocean side of the bridge because they could get killed in the traffic.

Among the nineteenth-century immigrants who sailed or stumbled to San Francisco was a Prussian named Adolph Sutro from the town, oddly enough, of Aix-La-Chapelle. Sutro joined the rush for silver in Nevada's Comstock Lode. After eighteen years of solid effort he devised a method of extracting ore from a mountain mine while simultaneously ventilating the shafts, a novel process that made him a fortune. When he sold his interest in the business he retired to San Francisco and embarked upon a political career, serving for several years as Reform Mayor of the City.

When he died in 1898 Sutro had left his signature all over the city. He planted a forest northwest of Twin Peaks in the 1870s which was steadily enlarged by schoolchildren. The land on which his now-vanished house once stood now contains a twenty-acre, thickly cultivated garden and park, which was donated to the city by his daughter. Marble statuary is mixed in with the gardens. These statues are handsome but not exactly museum pieces; they are Belgian in origin and were brought to San Francisco in ships which used them for ballast.

Across from Sutro Park is the Cliff House, a restaurant that has been in use since the 1860s. Cliff House overlooks the Pacific Ocean particularly the sharp pointed Seal Rocks on which sea lions playfully splash around. Cliff House has been through some pretty exciting times. A dynamite-laden ship blew up beneath it, nearly destroying it in 1887, then seven years later it burned down. It was rebuilt just in time for the quake and fire and burned down again. The present one was built in 1907, and is remodelled periodically. Sutro was the original owner of the structure.

Above, an unexpected view of the Golden Gate Bridge in a flowery setting.

12.

There are many other points of interest scattered about San Francisco's ocean front. Land's End is for lovers, a steep promontory with a romantic view of Mile Rock Lighthouse, several hundred feet offshore. To wards the marine shore is a piece of ocean nicknamed the Potato Patch, a non-humorous nickname given it by seamen who had had to navigate its treacherous waters.

Mount Davidson, in Mount Davidson Park, is the highest point in San Francisco. The summit holds a concrete and steel Easter cross some 103 feet high. The base contains a crypt with relics from the Holy Land, which was also the source of the water with which the concrete sealing the structure was mixed. Easter sunrise services are held annually here for thousands of people.

Perhaps the most spectacular building is the Palace of the Legion of Honor in Lincoln Park. It incorporates many design features of the original in Paris and reflects the contribution the French have made to the cultural life of the city. That contribution has been considerable. San Francisco boasts the oldest French newspaper in the West—the *Courrier Français des Etats.* There are innumerable French organizations, including *L'Alliance Française.* The Palace was designed by Bernard Maybeck for the Panama Pacific Exposition of World War One and inspired such astounded admiration that one poet Edwin Markham flatly called it the most beautiful structure built in the history of mankind.

Like so many of San Francisco's other buildings, the Palace has had a strange history. It stands on a site where the first laundries were established, in the mid-nineteenth century. By 1939 it was used as a storage depot for city equipment and had tennis courts installed in it. Maybeck designed it so that its arches, columns and galleries faced on a lagoon in memory of the Becklin painting "Island of the Dead". It was immensely popular but unfortunately the passage of years was not gentle to its structure. Its imitation Travertine marble was falling apart by the 1950s and there was continuous decay of pediments and statue details. Arms, legs, and heads fell merrily from the bodies onto the ground and a major renovation was clearly essential. The Palace has now been restored to its former considerable splendor.

The Palace is an art museum today, one of the very best west of the Mississippi. The permanent collection is a marvellous balance between old and new, inclusive of such painters as Constable, Monet and San Francisco's own Arthur Putnam. It has 19 galleries which also exhibit porcelain, tapestries, anti-

The tourist hardly expected this: the Museum of the Legion of Honor, a duplica of its counterpart in Paris, in Lincoln Park.

que furniture and within its walls are a little theatre and two enclosed gardens.

The building is U-shaped and contains a colonnaded courtyard with one of the five original bronze casts of Rodin's *The Thinker.* Even more impressive is its locale, which is one of nature's works of art. It overlooks the Golden Gate from a height of two hundred feet on the spot where Fernando Rivera y Moncado and Father Francisco Palou once erected a small wooden cross.

The section of San Francisco known as the "Western Addition" presses close to the Pacific shore west of the major hills. "Western Survivor" may be a more appropriate name, for this area completely escaped the great fire. It is the oldest of the large sections of San Francisco.

The Western Addition is the most ethnically mixed of all the city's parts. The bulk of the population today is Negro. Originally the Western Addition was a Jewish area. World War Two brought in huge numbers of laborers to work in the shipyards. At the end of the war, the construction industries cut back, leaving an overcrowded job market. Many neighborhoods suffered as a result.

More poignant was the fate of the Japanese Americans living in the area. In one of the country's most ill-conceived acts, large numbers of them were arrested and forcibly moved into relocation camps until the war hysteria died down. Thousands of Japanese were affected by this measure—one third of them American citizens. When they returned to San Francisco, they found their neighborhoods occupied by other people.

Japanese Americans represent the second largest non-white ethnic group in the state of California. In San Francisco alone it is estimated they account for over twelve thousand inhabitants. On Pine Street is a

*View of San Fran-
cisco State College.*

brand new Japan Center filled with shops, restaurants, a hotel and Kabuki theatre. The street also boasts the Hongwanji Buddhist Temple, the Nichiran Buddhist Church and St Francis Xavier Catholic church, named for the Missionary to Japan.

San Francisco's Russian area centers roughly around Sutter and Divisadero Streets. Most of the 37,000 Russians are descendants from the October Revolution and there are several bookshops as well as a Russian center in this neighborhood.

The University of San Francisco is technically a Jesuit Institution but is open to all denominations. It is a spectacularly handsome complex of Spanish Revival style dominated by a pair of tall, twin towers. The campus is 20 acres and the buildings are a beautiful pink tinged type of concrete which glitters under the California sun. The University started out as St Ignatius College in 1859 and the name was changed on the 75th anniversary of its founding. The school is coeducational and is noted for its law school. Combined with the San Francisco College for Women, San Francisco State College and the varied branches of the University of California, the city has come a long way since the founding, in 1848, of the Public Institute School, which was a dilapidated wreck of a building on Portsmouth Plaza, where instruction was provided for thirty or forty people.

The overview of the entire city at Twin Peaks in the southern section of San Francisco graphically shows this city in all its confusing and gorgeous variety. From the vantage-point of the figure-eight drive surmounting them, the city appears to roll and disappear in waves of earth, its neighborhoods and its secrets tucked away amongst the hills. One wonders sometimes if any

sense or organization can be made from it. The hills break up what would normally be considered a regular geographic development. To further madden the city student, Twin Peaks regularly blossoms with a wild, tangled profusion of rhododendrons, the colored petals and free lushness making one wonder if the city, which like all cities supposedly destroys Nature, really exists. San Francisco seems so insubstantial from here, and the more philosophically-minded observer might well wonder whether all the mightiest works of man are that way.

Incidentally, Twin Peaks are graphically described by the local Indian tribes. The Spanish call them *Los Pechos de la Choca*— the breasts of the Indian maiden. Despite the residential clutter that has disfigured them, the Twin Peaks give one a clearer view of the city's ambiance than any other point in the Bay Area.

One can finally get a tenuous grip on this diverse, vibrant city by simply watching the liquid shadows of the setting sun darkening gleaming buildings, section by section. In a burst of hubris, someone named a peak in this area as Mount Olympus and crowned its crest with the Liberty Monument, a sculpture portraying Liberty as a woman, with a male representing despotism at her feet. It is an incomplete sculpture: Liberty's torch and sword distracted seamen from the channel to the Golden Gate and so parts of the work were removed. The most notable interruption of the view from Twin Peaks is Buena Vista Hill rising like a sodden lump in the midst of the white buildings. Upon this hill is a large park and around its base cluster the German and Scandinavian sections of the city.

Tropical plants in Kew Gardens.

13.

It is a common criticism of American cities that they lack history. The effects of time passing, of generations of builders who have lived, flourished and died leaving certain personal traits that remain forever, give cities a sense of timelessness which some visitors say they find lacking in America. These combine with certain symbols—Paris's Arc de Triomphe, Berlin's lakes, London's Big Ben—to fix a given city's personality indelibly in one's mind.

There are obvious symbols for San Francisco—cable cars, the hills, the Golden Gate Bridge—that one thinks of when one hears the name spoken. Yet a good argument could be made for nominating Golden Gate Park as the most accurate representation of the city's personality. The Golden Gate Park strikes a visitor as a highly improbable phenomenon. It runs half a mile from mid-city to the Pacific shore and its one thousand seventeen acres of green, almost tropical lushness make it appear as though the march of civilization has somehow been reversed and a wilderness is forcing its way into the concrete and steel.

Parks became a necessity for cities in the nineteenth century when city planners realized the importance of open spaces. Some have suggested that since San Francisco already exists in a beautiful setting, it needed a park the way a jungle needs cultivating. Certainly its site was not very promising. "A dreary waste of shifting sandhills where a blade of grass cannot be raised without four posts to support it," was one dour, editorial reaction to the proposed site.

Building greenery on sand dunes would have taxed the ingenuity of an Einstein. John McLaren, the Scottish immigrant who fathered the park was not exactly an Einstein but one cannot help but feel he was a genius of some kind. He had worked as a caretaker on many garden estates in England where the natural look was becoming popular. McLaren spent months looking for a type of grass that would bind the sands together and, after much experimenting, settled for a European beach grass. He served as superintendent from 1887 to 1943 and it is said that, during his lifetime, he planted more than a million trees, including oaks, conifers, and over a hundred varieties of eucalyptus, not to mention innumerable flowers. Golden Gate Park is particularly famous for its rhododendrons. Some of McLaren's ideas were ignored. His strong dislike for statues most probably extended to buildings in general. He believed parks should be used by pedestrians: thus there are very few "Keep Off the Grass" signs.

McLaren's distaste for statues has been

ignored. The park is full of them, including one in honor of McLaren himself. Furthermore it is the home of many of the city's most distinguished cultural entities.

The Conservatory embodies McLaren's love of botany. The long glass enclosure is a replica of the Conservatory in Kew Gardens, London. Orchids of rare types are its specialty but its collection of ferns and oriental flora is outstanding. The displays change seasonally and, upon a large flower bed in front of the building, the plants are periodically arranged to spell out messages.

The M.H. DeYoung Museum is a complex of structures housing a tremendous variety of art. Various foundations and donors have endowed it with Rembrandts, Titians, El Grecos and works by other artists of a similar stature as well as separate collections of tapestries from Flanders and French 18th-Century furnishings. So continuous are the endowments that pour into it, that the museum is forced to expand each year. If there is one style of art for which it is famous it would probably be its collection of pre-Columbian artifacts, an extensive assortment of Mayan, Aztec and Inca works.

The DeYoung Museum is named after a newspaper editor named Michael H. DeYoung who had operated the California Pavilion at the Chicago Exposition of 1893. DeYoung devised a Midwinter Exposition for San Fran-

cisco which enraged McLaren because of the number of buildings which were put up. The Exposition was a huge success which drew thousands of people from all over the country.

Poor McLaren. The legions of statues now decorating the park probably break his sleep in the grave. Many of them are excellent works. The main drive is lined with them. Daniel Chester French built a handsome bronze figure of a Bostonian-turned-Californian named Thomas Starr King, who helped bring California into the Union during the Civil War. Rupert French did an exceptionally active rendering of Junipero Serra, founder of the Missions and even Don Quixote is represented, along with Sancho Panza, surrounding their creator Cervantes.

The last remains of the Midwinter Exposition is the Japanese tea garden at the park's eastern end. It has proven immensely popular with the citizens and has been expanded from a tea house to a three-acre area with miniature bridges, streams, secluded paths, a five-roofed pagoda and an eleven-foot statue of Bhuddha cast in Japan in 1790. The park is perfect for picnics and quiet lunches and for those who wish authenticity with their surroundings.

The California Academy of Sciences has extensive centers in the park. The Academy supports varied scientific expeditions and

published works, most of it centered around the flora and fauna of the Pacific basin. Some believe it has the best display of Australian reptiles and amphibians outside of that country. For those whose idea of a charming afternoon is to have their hair stood on end, the Academy offers a gloriously comprehensive selection of entomological specimens. Insects. Spiders. Centipedes. Those crawly, leggy denizens of the small world. And for those who wish to contemplate their own minuteness, the Academy's Planetarium projector is the first one designed and built solely in the United States. A visit to the Aquarium will please the micro and macro extremes of one's contemplative mind, with over five hundred different species of fish. Just outside it is a tank in which the California sea lions can be seen swimming about.

Among the profusion of waterbird lakes, paths and athletic fields there is one striking monument close to the shoreline. This is the explorer Ronald Amundsen's little ship the Gjoa, which he gave to the city in 1905 after a three-year Arctic voyage. Since it is slightly outside the park, its presence cannot possibly disturb McLaren's sleep.

14.

San Francisco's influence extends to its sister communities across the bay. Oakland is noted for its elaborately handsome system of city parks and museum complexes, and Berkeley is home to the famed University of California, whose towering Campanile bell tower looks out over the East Bay.

There are several islands in both the Bay and the seas adjacent to the city. The largest is Angel Island, District Headquarters of the Immigration and Naturalization Service. A lot of angels hover over it; the island was notorious for the number of duels fought on its ground, the most famous being an 1858 disagreement between a Senator and a Court Clerk over the question of slavery.

The Farallon Islands, 26 miles west of the mainland, have an unusual arrangement with the city. Although they are part of it, no one, not even an official, may set foot on them without permission of the lighthouse superintendent. Treasure Island in the Bay is an artificial enclave used by the Navy.

By far the most famous of the city's islands is "The Rock", known far and wide as Alcatraz, the Federal Penitentiary, which has been the permanent home of some of America's most unsociable citizens, such as George (Machine Gun) Kelly, Scarface Al Capone, Alvin Karpis, a veritable aristocracy of murderers, gang bosses, mafiosi and extortionists, all the prisoners whom the Government believed too dangerous to be housed in other areas. Alcatraz's most famous inmate may have been Robert Stroud who spent most of his life in solitary confinement. Convicted of the murder of a prostitute in Alaska and a guard at Leavenworth Kansas, Stroud embarked upon a study of bird pathology from his prison cell. Over a period of years, he acquired microscopes, slides, ornithology texts and dissection equipment in his cell, and began publishing his work all over the country. He became a recognized authority in this field and the nickname "Birdman of Alcatraz," made him one of the most famous convicts in the world.

It is true that no one ever successfully

Campus and life at Berkeley.

108

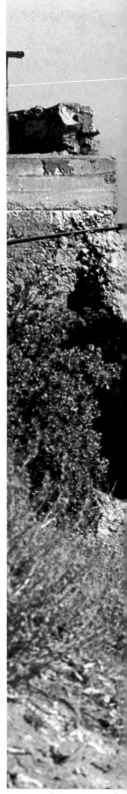

The delights of San Francisco itself are matched only by the beauty of its natural setting.

escaped from the prison. Alcatraz splits the riptides that roar in and out of the Golden Gate daily and those who managed to get out of the building perished in the bay. Yet coincidence or destiny seemed to decree that even Alcatraz not be totally escape-proof. The Justice Department closed the prison down in 1963. In its last days as a penitentiary, one man managed to get out and successfully crossed the bay to the mainland. He was recaptured immediately largely because the rigors of fighting the tides exhausted him. It was recommended by a commission that the island be turned over to the National Parks Service and that the prison be razed to the ground, and something more pleasant be raised there, perhaps a monument to the founding of the United Nations. Yet history suddenly descended upon the rock when a group of Indians laid claim to the island and moved onto its grounds, where they set up temporary housing and defied Government demands that they evacuate it. The island's status is still somewhat in limbo. One thing seems certain. It will survive whatever earthquakes Nature is said to have planned for the Bay Area; and if the past is any indication, it will take more than another April Misfortune to stop the City of the Golden Gate.